Amazon Echo:

Easy-to-Use Guide for Amazon Echo, Dot, and Tap

Table Of Contents

Introduction:

I want to thank you and congratulate you for downloading *Amazon Echo: Easy-to-Use Guide for Amazon Echo, Dot, and Tap.*

This book contains proven steps and strategies on how to most efficiently use your new Alexa powered Amazon device. There is no greater proof that we are living in a time of the future than with how incredibly powerful digital assistants have become.

Amazon's Alexa digital assistant is currently the market leader with an incredible understanding of natural human speech and holds the lead in a number of connected third-party apps and services. Alexa puts you in better control of your home and the features within.

I want to give you the information you need to get the most out of your Alexa powered device. Whether you're a tech wizard or a computer novice, this book offers useful tips and information on how to make sure you are using Alexa to her utmost potential.

Here's an inescapable fact: Amazon's Alexa is constantly being updated with new features and finding integration with the latest in third-party services. To stay current on Alexa and all the amazing things she can do you will need this book. There are tons of features that hiding just under the surface of your Amazon Echo powered device.

If you do not learn about all of the amazing features that Amazon's Alexa brings to the digital assistant marketplace, then you will be wasting a great deal of your brand new device's potential.

There is an opportunity here to have your house set up exactly as you always pictured it – a futuristic home where information and control are just a voice command away.

You took a leap of faith by purchasing an Echo powered device; now it's time to see the fruit of your purchase and learn about all of the truly incredible things Alexa can do for you.

It's time for you to jump start your home into the 21st century with the latest in digital technology. Using the power of the cloud and the tips in this book, Alexa will become a gateway to a better future with more control over your home, access to information at your fingertip, and entertainment that can be enjoyed for the entire household.

Come and join me as you learn about the simple tricks and the mind-bending features that Alexa holds!

Chapter 1: Basics of The Echo, Tap, and Dot

No matter the device that you purchase from Amazon, whether it's the Echo, Tap or Dot, you will be receiving the world's most advanced digital assistant.

Alexa is Amazon's answer to Microsoft's Cortana and Apple's Siri – she is a digital assistant that is miles ahead of the competition and has a much greater set of core abilities. Alexa's greatest strengths come in her ability to network with your home's lighting, thermostat, and more.

The difference between the Echo, Dot, and Tap lie in how they encase Alexa and how they gate access to her services.

Digital assistants are nothing new in the tech world. You are probably most familiar with Apple's Siri that first debuted on the iPhone 4S in 2011 and has grown more capable ever since. Still, the digital assistant has not brought about the great change that was promised in advertising campaigns and leaders in the tech world.

Siri has her uses, but overall the digital assistant is not effective enough to be used every day. A lot of this has to do with just *how* we access assistants like Siri and Cortana. For both assistants, the input lies on your phone. We carry our phones everywhere we go but reaching into your pocket to verbally command your phone to do something that you can just as quickly do in a few button presses simply not practical; it is not solving an existing problem.

This is where Alexa truly shines; not only does Alexa offer better integration with apps and services, but she is fundamentally more useful in that she is connected to your home. Alexa will never need to rest in your pocket, and you will never need to fish her out of your bag.

Once Alexa has been properly setup on any supported Echo device (Echo, Tap, Dot), she can register a user's commands from a great distance. The utility of requesting information at a moment's notice, without having to reach for your phone, cannot be understated. If you have been unimpressed with digital assistants before, think about how cumbersome their use was in that you had to be constantly reaching for your phone.

Now imagine simply speaking to your home and being able to get consistently the information you were seeking – this is the future that Alexa brings to your household. Your first task in integrating Alexa into your life is choosing how you will house your new assistant.

Alexa's Home In The Cloud

Alexa does not live inside of the Tap, Echo, or Dot, but is rather stored in the cloud. This means that Alexa can process voice requests with far greater precision due to the increase in power she is able to draw from cloud computing. As you make requests to Alexa, the information is being transmitted to Amazon and Amazon's computers can crunch the data much faster than any personal computer can.

This does mean that you will need a steady internet connection to use Alexa effectively, but in turn, you gain a massive increase in computing power and remove the fear of needing to upgrade Alexa in the future.

Alexa will constantly improve as she is enhanced on Amazon's servers and there is no purchase necessary to access these enhancements.

The choice you have to make is what type of hardware you want to hold Alexa. The hardware will determine the size that Alexa takes up in your home, the power draw she uses, and the clarity of the audio she emits and how well she can hear your own voice. Currently, Amazon offers three choices for consumers all coming at various price points; there is something for every shopper.

Amazon Echo

The Amazon Echo is the marquee Echo device that Amazon has been selling for the longest amount of time. This product comes in at $179.99 and is the best product for consumers that want high-quality audio and the best audio pickup for taking requests from all over your home.

The Echo has a large cylindrical form factor with a speaker that wraps 360 degrees around the entire body of the device. There are no displays on the device, and everything is handled with your voice. The only exception to this is the initial setup which is handled through your iOS or Android device.

Picture courtesy of Amazon.com

The Echo is the most expensive Alexa device for your home, but it is also comes packed with the best quality speakers and recording pickups.

If you are looking for a device for your living room or kitchen, this is probably what you are going to want to buy.

The price is a little bit steep, but unlike tablets and Amazon's other devices like the Kindle, the core of the Echo is entirely software based and updates will come for years and will always be free. The main upgrades that will come to the Echo in future hardware revisions will be more impressive recorders and better speakers, but as far as the tech world is concerned, audio hardware will not have the massive improvements that other tech devices receive after only a few years.

Echo Dot

The Amazon Dot, commonly referred to as the Echo Dot, is a smaller more compact version of its larger brother. The Dot has a fantastically slim form factor that can fit on just about anywhere. When this product initially came out, there was actually quite a bit of confusion as to how it fit into the entire Echo ecosystem.

Due to some slight brand confusion, it was once thought that a regular Amazon Echo was required to use the Echo Dot – this is not true however and the Echo Dot can be used entirely independently from the larger Amazon Echo.

The Echo Dot is the most compact Amazon device featuring Alexa but still requires a standard power outlet and is for use strictly inside the home. The small form factor means a less powerful speaker and receiver, but don't be fooled; the Dot can still be heard from a great distance and can pick up your voice from across a large room.

Packing the same power as the larger Echo, the main difference in the Dot comes in its philosophy of use.

If the larger Echo was designed for use in one large room, then the Echo Dot was designed to be placed in multiple rooms all across your house.

The lower price point of $89.99 makes the Echo Dot more appealing if you plan on filling your home with multiple Echo devices, but know that each device functions independently from one another.

This means that while each Echo might be connected to the same services throughout your home, having two Echo Dots next to each and asking Alexa a question will be met with the same answer coming from two different devices.

An ideal use of the Echo Dot is placing them in rooms where your voice won't be picked up on the other device.

Currently, the Echo Dot is the most popular Alexa supported device. The price point is appealing to a wide variety of consumers, and the form factor fits in nicely with just about any room in the house.

The Echo Dot could originally only be purchased if you already had an Amazon Echo or if you knew someone that had one. As the device starts to come back in stock, it's possible orders made through other Echo devices will be given priority, so if you are desperate for an Echo Dot you may want to try asking your friend's Alexa to order one.

It will come through your friend's account, but this is currently the fastest way of securing an Echo Dot. To place an order, simply ask Alexa to "Order an Echo Dot."

Amazon Tap

The Amazon Tap is the second iteration of Echo devices and is designed as an Alexa on the go. It's best to think about the Amazon Tap as a Bluetooth speaker that happens to come with Alexa as a digital assistant.

While this means that you can use the Amazon Tap outside of the home, the device also has significantly lower audio quality than the other Amazon Echo devices and is less feature rich in hardware.

To gain access to Alexa, you must *tap* the device and cannot merely call out to Alexa. This makes the way that you interact with the Tap much more in line with how most users use Siri or Cortana.

Picture courtesy of Wired.com

The Amazon Tap comes in at $130 but is frequently discounted and sold for as little as $110. The device has all of the trappings of its two siblings, but its initial design as a Bluetooth speaker is quite apparent.

It seems as though the designers were creating a portable speaker device for Amazon and the Alexa features were added towards the end of development. This is made evident by how the user is forced to *tap* the device to access Alexa.

The positives of the Amazon Tap are that it is fully wireless and can run up to nine hours on battery power. This puts the device in line with other Bluetooth speakers regarding battery life, but its price point is on the more expensive side for these types of devices.

The main purpose of the Tap is to amplify audio coming out of your smartphone, and it does this to decent success. The audio quality is good, but it isn't great.

If you are looking for a dedicated Bluetooth speaker there are better and cheaper devices, and as far as Alexa powered devices go the other choices offer potentially better usability due to voice controls.

This is, however, the one Echo device that works on the go. If Alexa becomes a major part of your life, then it could be worthwhile bringing the Amazon Tap with you as you travel.

Chapter 2: Which Device Is Right For You?

There are several different price points for Echo devices and depending on what you are seeking; there is going to be an appropriate choice just for you.

You must remember that the main selling point of all Echo devices is the Alexa digital assistant and each Echo device has the same level of performance when it comes to tasks that Alexa will handle.

Since Alexa's computations are done on a remote server, the speed of responses will largely be the same across devices, with major changes in variability coming from the quality of your internet connection.

In terms of bandwidth however Alexa is quite light on resources, and you shouldn't have any problems unless you are using an ADSL or satellite connection.

The main differentiator across Echo devices is then the form factor and quality of the speakers and recording devices on each product, as well as the price of each product.

Each device has their own pros and cons but in essence, you are receiving the same experience regardless of the product you choose. Keep this in mind as you shop and you should be able to find a device that fits your needs and works within your budget.

Amazon Echo

At $179.99 the Amazon Echo is the most expensive in the Echo line of devices, but it is also the most feature rich. Coming packed with the most powerful speaker system of the three and the best range on its built-in recorder, the Echo is great for family rooms and parts of the house where you are likely to get a lot of foot traffic.

This model is great for playing music at parties or answering simple conversion question in a kitchen. Its place in larger rooms where the whole family spends time makes it also able to adapt to each member of the family, getting more familiar with each voice and being able to pinpoint what a family member is saying, even if they have a heavy accent.

The cost and size of this device are its main detractors, and if you are looking for an Echo device for your bedroom, there are better choices.

Also while the speaker quality is quite good, audiophiles will likely want to set up external speakers to get the best quality audio. Serving the purpose of large family rooms, the pickup of the recording device on the original Echo is quite strong, and while you can disable the recorder entirely, if you are worried about surveillance or setting Alexa off accidently, this model will have the greatest listening range of the three.

Lastly, if a new hardware revision for any Echo device is going to arrive soon, it will first arrive for this model. While the Echo is still very new, and if you are interested in one I do think you should pick one up now, the original Echo is the oldest device, and so it will likely see the first hardware revision. Again since Alexa is powered by the cloud, this does not mean a faster device necessarily, but you can probably expect slightly better speakers and a more capable microphone, as well as a possible price cut if manufacturing gets cheaper.

Echo Dot

Personally this is my favorite Echo Device – there are pieces of hardware that you hold that really make you feel like you are in the future. The last time I experienced this feeling prior to the Echo Dot was with the original iPhone.

The power of Alexa rests in the cloud, and the Echo Dot uses this to its advantage by being the smallest Echo device available. It fits great on any table, and its elegant design makes it easy on the eyes. The recorder and speakers on the deice, while not as powerful as the full-sized Echo, are quite good and have excellent range in small to medium sized rooms.

The price point is also the most affordable at $89.99, giving you an incentive to add more to your home if you find that you would like to use Alexa in different parts of your house. The feature set is exactly the same as the other Echo devices, and Alexa can connect to your home and manage all of the same systems.

As the Echo Dot originally rolled out there was quite a bit of confusion as to how it functions with other Echo products in your home. This is largely due to how orders were first placed for the Echo Dot.

Originally orders could only be placed through the first Amazon Echo, and so the Dot was thought of as a companion device. It was stated in Chapter One, but it's important to note that the Echo Dot is a stand alone device, and you do not need any other Echo products to get all of its functionality.

The main negative to the Echo Dot is it is currently impossible to find. Alexa and the Amazon Echo are great ideas, but the original price point was a little bit too much for consumers that were on the edge.

The Echo Dot seems to have found the right price point to allure a great number of consumers, but unfortunately the manufacturing and supply chain on parts has left many of consumers without anyway of ordering the product.

If you are interested in the Echo Dot, be on the lookout for when Amazon starts shipping them again. It's possible that Amazon will lock orders behind a Prime membership, as they have done with other Echo devices in the past, but know that Amazon Prime offers several apps that will heighten your experience with any Echo device.

While it is doubtful that when orders for the Dot open up again, they will only be taken on other Echo devices, this is something to keep in mind, and you may want to track down a friend that already has an Echo. When the Echo Dot becomes available ordering a Dot through your friend's Echo might be the bet way to ensure receiving the product.

Amazon Tap

The Amazon Tap is an overall difficult product to recommend. It seems like a device that was changed several times through development, and the overall product is less than impressive.

If you are looking for an Alexa powered device that you can take with you outside of the home, then the Amazon Tap is the best option. Running on battery power, the Tap can provide nine hours of audio and cloud integration ensures the Alexa is just as fast on the Tap as it is on any other Echo product. The drawbacks of the device, however, might be a little bit too much to justify a purchase and the relatively heavy price tag it carries.

At $130 the Amazon Tap is neither a great Bluetooth speaker nor the best Alexa powered device. Standing somewhere in the middle between these two devices the Tap comes with a lot of drawbacks that hampers the whole experience.

Communication with Alexa is not done through voice communication but by hitting a button on the device and so it will have to be close by to use the digital assistant. The battery life at nine hours might seem impressive, but as far as

Bluetooth speakers go, the audio quality does not justify the nine hours of battery draw. The audio is murky in the best of conditions and some genres of music can sounds flat out bad through its low voltage speakers.

On the bright side, the microphone is quite good at picking up your voice after you've *tapped* the device. The price point of $130 might seem a little bit steep, but it is currently the cheapest Echo device that can easily be found.

I wouldn't expect Amazon to continue the Tap line of products in the future. In a lot of ways, this seems like a fluke product and the Tap name is so ingrained with Alexa being locked behind a button that chances of a follow-up under the same branding are slim.

This does mean you should not buy the Tap if the feature set is exactly what you want, but you should probably purchase one now before production stops. In terms of software and firmware updates Amazon has stated that they will stand behind the Tap, however it seems likely that updates for the Tap will be discontinued before other more popular Echo products.

Chapter 3: Your New Digital Assistant (Basic Tasks)

You've chosen your Amazon Echo device, and you are ready to be acquainted with your new digital assistant, Alexa. Alexa is voice activated on the Amazon Dot and Amazon Echo – by simply using the key phrase "Alexa", the Echo will wake from its sleep and be ready for a wide variety of inputs.

These requests can range from simple tasks to complicated multi-step dialogues. A lot of the fun with Alexa comes from experimentation and seeing just how natural she can act. Don't be afraid to try commands even if they aren't listed in this book.

What I really want you to gain is understand how Alexa uses information and some of the great uses that she can have in your home. In this chapter I will simply be discussing Alexa as if she was connected to your home network and no third party applications were loaded. This is what Alexa can do out of the box and once your Echo device has been set up.

Setup

You'll notice that your Amazon Echo does not have a display. Setting up your device and your account information is handled on your iOS or Android device. Simply download the Alexa app from the App Store or Google Play store, plug in your Echo device, and look for the settings under your Alexa app. The app will control your Echo device and dictate which wireless network to connect to.

I know that you've probably connected devices to your wireless network before, and the Echo is largely the same, but there is one key difference you will want to take note of. Alexa does not need a lot of bandwidth or data to function as best she can, but she does need a very low latency connection with minimal packet loss. This might sound very technical, and that's OK – what we are trying to do here is make sure that Alex has the most *stable* connection, not necessarily the *fastest* connection.

If you are living in an apartment, I suggest using the 5 GHz band that Alexa supports as most routers now come with this as a standard feature. The 5 GHz frequency is above the frequency that most other devices use, and you will run into less interference. If you are living in a home or if you are placing your Echo far away from your wireless access point, you'll want to use the 2.4 GHz band as this can be used from a further distance. Again, do not worry about the speed of Alexa butt rather just the consistently in her connection.

Privacy

Unless you are using the Amazon Tap, your Echo device Alexa will constantly be listening for her activation phrase. This does not mean that Alexa is processing your every word, but it does mean that she is constantly drawing power and on the lookout for her name. The moment Alexa hears "Alexa," she will begin to process your next sentence and seek to give you an answer. This is the main selling point of Alexa, but there may be times when you want to avoid Alexa from listening for her activation phrase, whether it be a business meeting or a romantic evening with a significant other. To turn off Alexa's recorder simply hold down the noise cancellation button on the top of the Echo device. You will want to press this button until a red circle lights up on the top of the cylinder. You cannot disable this setting through your voice and will have to press the button again to enable Alexa.

Natural Language

Alexa is the first digital assistant that *actually* works. Siri and Cortana have functionality, but so many of their answers rely on the quality of the question. Alexa is much smarter than other digital assistants and is great at parsing natural language.

You will always need the initial activation phrase to start Alexa, but after this feel free to speak naturally. This includes following up questions as Alexa will remember the topic at hand and you will not need to define the subject matter again.

If you are curious about "Who won the World Series in 1954?" Alexa would answer and any other query about World Series winners could be asked with "What about in 19xx?" If you ever miss a response that Alexa provides, you can simply say "Alexa can you repeat that?" and she will default to giving you the answer to your last question. Experiment and try different ways of asking questions; the point here is you don't need to speak with Alexa as she is simply a Google search tool.

Uses In The Kitchen

It's best to think about Alexa as a guide to the internet. She can relay most pieces of information from recipes to sports scores, but she can also do many of the simple functions that you might use Google for. A great use of Alexa is in her powerful conversion tools. If you find yourself in the kitchen and unsure of how many tablespoons of butter you need because the recipe measures the ingredient in cups, then simply ask Alexa to convert between cups and tablespoons. This can be done in specific amounts as well such as "3 cups to tablespoons".

Alexa can also be quite handy when a Google search can fix your recipe. If you've ever found yourself out of vanilla extract and preparing to wash yourself off before you sit down at a computer to look for a substitute, Alexa can help with that. Alexa is great at reading the information on results and for simple questions like these, she can inform you of a substitute without you needing to waste time washing your hands and going to your desktop.

Chapter Five will go more in depth on third party services, but Alexa has recently been upgraded to interact with the latest in smart refrigerators. Currently, these are limited to Samsung brand refrigerators, but features like recipe meal ideas based on the ingredients in your fridge is possible. The information that Alexa is drawing from is entirely from your refrigerator and the quality of the recipes currently rests in the hands of Samsung.

Your Kids And Alexa

Perhaps I'm old-fashioned, but as a child, in elementary school, I remember going home and doing my homework at the kitchen table. I would constantly pester my mother by asking her spelling questions and history questions while she was working away at household chores. If your child does homework in the same room that your Amazon Echo sits, you will want to introduce them to Alexa.

Your children will have to use the same key phrase of "Alexa" before every question, but Alexa is great for all types of basic school questions. For fun, you can also ask Alexa to provide you or your child with questions. If you ask Alexa for a "spelling bee word," she will ask you to spell a word and tell you if you are correct.

Alexa is prepared to handle questions ranging from math to spelling, to geography, and everything in-between. Having your child use Alexa gives them a tool to quickly and accurately get a response to every question no matter how big or small.

Alexa also has the great advantage of you being to hear your children's inquiries. If you moderate how much internet usage your child gets, this can be a great help. You'll know that their online searches are related to schoolwork because you will actually hear their requests.

Chapter 4: Music and Entertainment Through Alexa

The power of Alexa comes in her ability to sync with different apps and services across a variety of media. By and far the single most useful media type is audio, and Alexa provides a great way to listen to audiobooks, podcasts, and music. Alexa does not need a specific request to get started and will respond to a general query for music, or even a specific genre of music.

Issuing the command "Alexa, play some classic rock" will create a playlist and start playing from any sources that hold music of this genre. Depending on when or if you started to collect digital music, how you listen and what apps you use is gong to be slightly different.

Listening To The Music You Own

Any music that you have purchased through Amazon will be stored on your prime account and can be easily accessed using Alexa. However, I have found that most of the music I listen to through Alexa is my own. This means MP3s that I have gathered over the years and have uploaded to Amazon's music streaming service.

Now if you are above a certain age of around forty or below a certain age of about twenty-five, then you are likely only using streaming services, but there are many of us in the middle that came of age to the internet during the time of Napster, Morpheus, and the CD ripping subculture. If any of this sounds familiar, then there is a good chance that you are sitting on several gigabytes of music. For absolutely free, you can upload up to 250 of your own MP3s and play them back on any Amazon device, including all Amazon Echo products. If you are holding onto more songs, then a yearly fee of $24.99 is required to upload up to 250,000 songs. This should be enough space to upload your entire collection, and remember now with these songs in the cloud they can be played back from any device and anywhere as long as you have an internet connection. It should be noted that this music can only be played back if the corresponding profile is signed into Alexa.

Switching User Accounts

For all of your digital purchases through Amazon, whether audiobooks or music, this will always be tied to your account and you will always have access to this content. It's likely that in your household you have multiple Amazon accounts and will need to set up multiple profiles on your Echo device.

To do this, you will want to open the Alexa app on your smartphone and go to "settings", "accounts", and then "add user account". Alexa is only able to playback content that has been purchased on the currently singed in profile. While this may sound complicated, switching profiles are quite easy, and the only time investment is setting up multiple accounts using the Alexa app.

Once you have setup your user profiles on Alexa, you'll find an easy time switching between profiles. Simply say "Alexa account" and Alexa will ask what user account you want to log into. If you are unsure of the account that is currently logged in, simply ask "Alexa what account is currently logged in?" Remember that Alexa is great at natural language and that there are various phrases you can use to switch accounts, so you don't need to worry about providing a specific phrase for each request.

The Available Music Apps

Currently, the Amazon Echo supports a wide range of streaming services. The most notably absent service is iTunes, but this is to be expected with an Amazon device. If you are interested in having your purchases on iTunes play through Alexa, you can use a workaround and upload your MP3s to Amazon's music store – for more information see *Listening To The Music You Own*.

The available services are listed below. Each service can be added to the Echo by opening the Alexa app on your smartphone and adding individual music apps.

- Amazon Music
- Prime Music
- Spotify Premium
- Pandora
- TuneIn
- iHeartRadio
- Audible

It is on your smartphone that you will always sign into music services. You should note that currently, music services are on an account level, so if you pay for a Spotify premium subscription, you will have to be signed into the corresponding Amazon account where you linked your Spotify information. Switching profiles will leave you without access to the Spotify account. It has been a long requested feature that music services not be tied to accounts, and this feature will likely be included in a software update.

Picture courtesy of Cnet.com

Making A Purchase With Your Voice

If you are heavily involved in the Amazon eco system, making a purchase through your Echo can be a fast way to get what you need with a simple voice command. I have found that most purchases I make through my Echo are audiobooks, songs, and albums, but you can also purchase other items and even reorder past orders all through Alexa. To allow voice purchasing go into "settings," "accounts," "authorize voice purchases" and then follow the instructions on your Alexa app through your smartphone.

Alexa will make sure that she can recognize your voice, so accidental purchases don't happen. This has saved me quite a few times when my kids attempt to order Minecraft music through our Echo.

Chapter 5: Controlling Your Home

Amazon Echo devices are constantly evolving how they interact with your home. Just this year a partnership was announced with the new line of Samsung refrigerators, and when set up, Alexa can let you know about every item in your fridge.

She will even give you recipes based on what you have in stock or recommend purchases for your next outing to the supermarket.

As it currently stands, however, there are many ways to integrate Alexa into your home, offering you more control that can be accessed with simple voice commands.

Lighting

The best way to control atmospheric lighting in your home is through Phillip's Hue products and their integration with Alexa. After installing the lighting throughout your home, the lights will communicate via Bluetooth or through your wifi network (depending on the version of lights you buy).

Using the Philip's Hue application on your phone to set different light profiles, you can then activate a profile using Alexa.

This is a great way to bring your home into the 21st century with not only voice-activated lights but with subtle changes to lighting that can alter the mood of any room in your house.

This feature works with all Echo devices and can control lights that are not in the same room as the Echo device you are using.

You may want to keep this in mind if you have children as they have a habit of using some of these more advanced features to play pranks.

If it ever becomes a problem you can simply go into user accounts and make it so that light commands only work when controlled with certain voices. You can program you and your significant other's voices so that only you have access. Note that in this scenario guests would not be able to control the lighting. It is expected that in an upcoming patch you will simply be able to block certain voices and allow all others, however at the time of this book this feature is still absent, so be mindful whom you want to lock out of control.

There are alternatives to Philip's Hue products, and these are being added all the time. I have a friend that has his entire home wired using Insteon products for the thermostat, lighting, and ceiling fan control.

Alexa will work with each of these products and be able to control them independently. While the software from Philips and Insteon is absolutely stellar, you will want to look into how each individual product works before making a purchase.

Also less known brands do not necessary mean worse quality, but it does almost certainly mean less support in the future – this is not at the feet of Amazon but rather the company that updates the software for their products.

Alexa will always work with a product in the same way, but unless a company updates their profiles for Alexa, new functionally may not cross over in future updates.

Outlets

A much more cost efficient way to control the lighting in your house, or any electronic system, is through Belkin's WeMo product line. A WeMo simply plugs into your existing outlet and acts as a switch that is controlled over wifi. By going into the settings for Alexa, you can add this third party service. The main programming is done using the WeMo app, and key phrases are then set up on Alexa.

I currently use this system in my home to control the lighting in my den and dining room and to turn on and off my entertainment center. I found the voice controls for third party apps do not work as well with natural langue so you'll want to be careful what keywords you program.

For my wife and I, we had to program both "light group three" and "light three" into the accepted keywords to get both to register.

You can have phrases for the same function, so don't worry about overlapping commands. You'll just want to make sure that you have programmed each keyword that you think you will use.

In terms of the cost, I found WeMo to be the best value for controlling nonspecific functions throughout our home.

The average WeMo will run you $40, but sales are fairly frequent, and I was able to buy several at around $30 each. While I only use the WeMo to control the lighting and entertainment system in my house, there is no technical reason it cannot be used to control anything that plugs into an outlet.

Some ideas for potential uses is controlling outside patio lighting, turning on and off a pool heater, or managing energy expenses if you use an in-window air conditioning unit.

Thermostat

There are quite a few thermostats that work with Alexa and they mostly all function the same way.

While Alexa adds a new way to interact with your thermostat it does not replace its basic functionality, so if there is a feature that doesn't exist on your thermostat then do not expect Alexa to control that aspect.

For example, some of the more budget thermostats do not offer wattage controls where a thermostat will modify the temperature based on how much power you want to consume. If this feature is not built into the thermostat itself, then it will not work with Alexa.

There are only three brands of thermostat that I would recommend: Sensi, Insteon, and Nest. Sensi and Insteon are both affordable and a great value at around $100, but lack some of the learning features of the more expensive Nest brand at $250.

If you are concerned about power usage, then Nest is the brand to go with as their learning software is currently the best on the market and has been shown to greatly reduce energy costs.

Alexa will work the same way with all of these systems and commands to Alexa will simply relay to the app and then to the thermostat.

Chapter 6: Personal Trainer, Alarm Clock, and More

How you use the Alexa is going to be dependent very much on the needs you have in your home. I do suggest that you try and use Alexa in a variety of situations to see what works best for you.

Every month new product integration is being added to Alexa – Amazon has taken to calling these features "skills." I use the following features nearly every single day, and without fail they make me feel like I am living in the future. Try these features and you too might fall in love with how easy Alexa can make certain tasks

Car Services

Both Uber and Lyft are supported on Alexa. By simply asking "Alexa can you get me an Uber/Lyft?", One will arrive at your door in just a few minutes. I love this feature and have found it much easier than reaching for my phone and using either app.

You will need to go into the settings of your Echo using the Alexa app and add a device location, so drivers know where to pick you up. As you request a driver, Alexa will inform you of how far away the driver is and at what time you can expect the driver to arrive.

Exercise Routine

If you ask Alexa for an exercise routine, she will provide an intense seven-minute workout. This is a free third party skill that can be added by simply requesting a workout. Most skills such as these simply need a keyword, and they will be downloaded and installed on your Echo device instantly.

The workout routine has already seen several updates and will provide you with a variety of different workouts

Alarm Clock and Calendar

It's quite a simple feature, but Alexa's alarm clock is invaluable. Asking Alexa to set an alarm for five minutes is a feature I use every night as I cook. The calendar function is also quite impressive as Alexa can interpret two dates and give the number of days in-between.

If you ask Alexa "How many days are between now and January 1st?" she will be able to interpret that you mean January of next year and be able to calculate the number of days instantly. I use this feature when I quickly need to know how many weeks are before a certain date.

Alexa comes pre-programmed with dates for Holidays as well, so you can try asking for the number of days until Christmas and she will provide the appropriate response.

Picture courtesy of Wareable.com

Trivia and Easter Eggs

The programmers at Amazon have equipped Alexa with an absolute trove of trivia and a ton of Easter Eggs. The list is too long to display here, but I suggest you try asking Alexa all sort of trivia questions.

Most answers are pre-programmed, but she is also able to produce an answer using Google search results. As for Easter Eggs, Alexa is best used when asked for information about famous robots.

If you ask her about Skynet or the Hal 9000, she will certainly have something to say. Unlike Siri, there are thousands of Easter Eggs hidden away in Alexa's programming.

I love to ask Alexa all types of questions just to see if she has a funny response or a clever answer. When your new Echo device arrives, try saying "Alexa, I am your father" – not only will she have a great quip, but she has dozens of responses that are all relevant and funny.

Conclusion:

Thank you again for downloading *Amazon Echo: Easy-to-Use Guide for Amazon Echo, Dot, and Tap.*

I hope this book was able to help you select the Echo device that is right for you and to get you acquainted with all of the incredible things Alexa is capable of. Regardless of the Echo device that you decided on, the real achievement is in Alexa and how capable of a digital assistant she is. I hope that she will be as impactful on your life as she has been on mine. So many technologies promise a glimpse of the future, but ever since I connected my home to Alexa, I feel like that promise has finally been met.

The next step is to setup your Amazon Echo device and to start experimenting with Alexa. Make sure to connect Alexa to all of your favorite streaming services and to be constantly on the lookout for new skills. Your Echo device is one that will grow better over time so make sure stay up to date with all of the amazing things Alexa can do.

Finally, if you enjoyed this book, please take the time to share your thoughts and post a review on Amazon. It'd be greatly appreciated!

Thank you and good luck!

www.ingramcontent.com/pod-product-compliance
Lightning Source LLC
Chambersburg PA
CBHW070238290526
45789CB00004B/1676